Macro Practice Skills

Macro Practice Skills

A STEP-BY-STEP GUIDE

JAN M. IVERY

GEORGIA STATE UNIVERSITY

cognella®
SAN DIEGO

Bassim Hamadeh, CEO and Publisher
Amy Smith, Project Editor
Abbey Hastings, Associate Production Editor
Emely Villavicencio, Senior Graphic Designer
Stephanie Kohl, Licensing Associate
Natalie Piccotti, Director of Marketing
Kassie Graves, Vice President of Editorial
Jamie Giganti, Director of Academic Publishing

cognella® | ACADEMIC PUBLISHING
3970 Sorrento Valley Blvd., Ste. 500, San Diego, CA 92121

BRIEF CONTENTS

CONTENTS

CHAPTER 1

Overview of the Generalist Social Work Practice Model

S ocial work is a dynamic and diverse profession that works with individuals, families, organizations, and communities. In order for social workers to effectively intervene across and within client populations, they need to be equipped with general skills and knowledge that can be applied at micro, mezzo, and macro system levels. Generalist practice is an ecological systems perspective for understanding clients within their social context. Since this is a broad systems approach to practice, the process used to examine the client's situation can be adapted for use in different settings. In social work, clients are not only individuals. They can be families, organizations, communities, and institutions. For example, generalist practice can be used to examine patterns of behavior within a family system to improve overall functioning as well as how an organization functions so that it reflects its mission and achieves its goals for service delivery.

Social work roles that are associated with generalist practice include broker, advocate, educator, and organizer. These roles are not specific to the level of intervention and can be applied in both micro and macro practice. In addition, the skills that are learned for generalist practice can be used when working with larger systems beyond the individual. Relationship and engagement, organization and group management, critical analysis, strategy and politics, and administration and management are skills that are necessary for macro social work practice (Reisch, 2018). These skills align with the generalist practice model.

The generalist practice model organizes key social work tasks that are essential to practice into six stages: engagement, assessment, planning, implementation, evaluation, and termination/follow-up. These stages are interrelated because the build on each other to progress to the next stage. Although they are presented as distinct stages, they are part of a fluid process, and it is not uncommon to revisit a stage if additional work is needed to move the client through the change process.

The first stage of the model is **engagement**. Engagement is a process that facilitates relationship building through the use of active listening and attending skills to build rapport with clients. Specific relationship and engagement skills during this stage include using open-ended questions to focus on the client's feelings and thoughts. This stage is focused on making initial observations about the information provided, behavior, and non-verbal cues. The ability to communicate effectively and meaningfully with diverse populations, to demonstrate directness and honesty, and to handle conflict, anger, resistance, and failure are examples of how relationship and engagement skills can be applied within the context of macro practice. This stage can be thought of as the "getting to know you" stage of the professional relationship. Since this occurs early in the partnership, emphasis should be placed on the expectations and guidelines for the professional relationship with the individual, group, or community.

Once the initial rapport is established, the social worker must begin to develop an initial idea of the current situation or presenting problem and the factors that are contributing to it. This is the **assessment** stage of the model. Although the focus is on articulating a clear statement of the need, problem, or situation, the social worker should also identify the client's strengths that can used during the intervention stage. This stage can be that part of process in which the social worker begins to the "put the pieces of the puzzle" together to see how different parts of the client's system interact. For macro practice, the organizational or group management skills during this stage are identifying problems, articulating the issues and developing specific goals from multiple stakeholders with diverse interests and needs (Reisch, 2018).

Planning is next stage. This is where the social worker will move from information gathering and observation to putting together a tentative plan for action. During this stage, specific goals, objectives, and action steps are created as the "roadmap" for how the social worker will work with the client. Analytic skills are essential during this stage to analyze the assessment data and identify areas where additional data are needed, incorporate a plan for evaluation, conduct a power analysis of the situation or problem, and select appropriate strategies (Reisch, 2018). Usually, a formal contact with the client that outlines the expectations and responsibilities for both the client and the social worker is created during this stage. In macro practice, a formal partnership agreement or memorandum of understanding (MOA) may be used instead of a client contact. Either way, the tasks that need to be completed, by whom, how, and where will need to be specified for each strategy so that everyone involved knows their role and how they will contribute. Macro social workers can apply their assessment skills to operationalize goals into program activities; establish and maintain group structure; plan and conduct conferences, events, and meetings; and prioritize and balance competing concerns and demands (Reisch, 20189).

Once an initial plan is created, the next stage is **implementation**: putting the plan into action. During this action oriented and dynamic stage, the main focus is following the plan and monitoring progress toward identified goals. It is important to note that it is not unusual to revise the plan as necessary in response to changes in the client's situation. In macro practice, internal (i.e., stakeholders, group structure) and external influences (i.e., economic changes, politics) can influence implementation. Thus, the macro social worker's strategic, political, and administrative administrative skills can be applied during this stage of the generalist model. Strategic and political skills reflect the social worker's ability to assess the interests and commitments of different stakeholder groups; continuously identify sources of power and minimize the threat of adversaries; facilitate group processes that will promote cohesion and collaboration within one's group, organization, and constituency while working as part of larger coalitions; and identify and address conflict and use persuasive communication (written and verbal) to tailor how their ideas are presented to diverse audiences and stakeholders groups (Reisch, 2018. Macro practice administrative and management skills are needed in this stage to provide oversight to the organizational and community-focused activities. These skills are necessary to match the activities in the plan with the appropriate resources (development and allocation), facilitate group decision making andestablish effective working relationships that respect differences. Time managementand maintaining records, minutes, and reports for accountability are necessary keep the strategy focused and on-task (2019).

Evaluation, the fifth stage of the model, is how social workers can determine to what extent the treatment goals have been achieved. Although evaluation is presented late in the model, it should be addressed in earlier discussions about goals so that the specific outcomes that will be assessed will be clearly defined. Evaluation examples include measures of changes in behavior, skills, and attitudes as the result of interventions and client satisfaction surveys. In macro practice, the analytic skills can be used to not only evaluate goal/task achievement but also the processes used to implement the strategy. By assessing both tasks and process goals, social workers can gain insight into what characteristics of the strategy (i.e., working relationships, resource allocation, conflict management, and communication) facilitated or hindered outcomes.

Termination/follow-up is the point the in model in which the professional relationship ends. The decision to terminate is based on when the treatment goals are achieved, if the client is able to problem solve without the assistance of formal services, if the client may need services from a different provider, and in some cases if the client feels he or she no longer needs the social worker. Termination is a period of transition and the social worker should make appropriate referrals for follow-up or additional services. It is important to be mindful of how clients react to this change and resolve any emotional reactions such as fear and anxiety that may result as they consider how they will implement what they have learned from their time spent receiving services and feeling like they are on their own. Similar to generalist practice, termination occurs in macro practice when the goals have been achieved. However, macro-focused projects, coalitions, and advocacy efforts may be more time limited, and termination is planned for from the initial planning. For example, if a group is organizing to advocate for a specific law, it knows that this strategy will "end" when it is passed or at the end of the legislative session.

Generalist Practice Model: Stages and Processes	
Engagement	Facilitate relationship development and build rapport with clients/ key stakeholders.
Assessment	Develop an initial idea of the factors that contribute to the current situation or presenting problem.
Planning	Use the information from the assessment to develop a tentative plan for action with clearly defined goals.
Implementation	Follow through on the action plan and monitor progress toward goal achievement.
Evaluation	Evaluate progress toward goal achievement and the processes used to implement the strategy.
Termination/follow-up	Formally end the formal professional relationship and make appropriate referrals for follow-up or transition.

APPLYING THE GENERALIST MODEL: AN EXAMPLE

Simone works for a nonprofit organization that provides supportive services for older adults in the community so they can remain in their homes as they age in place. The organization provides transportation, home repair services, and activities to reduce social isolation such as nutrition classes, shopping trips, and bingo. The organization has previously worked with the local housing authority to develop programs for the residents in the senior high rise. The housing authority has experienced increased complaints about the type and quality of the social programs they offer their residents. The housing authority would like to work with Simone's organization to further explore the residents' concerns. Simone's director asked her to lead this project to identify what needs to be done about services that are currently offered. Her application of the generalist model is outlined next:

Engagement: She scheduled a lunch meeting with the residents to introduce herself to them and explain why she was working with the housing authority. Although some of the residents expressed their concerns to her, some were still reluctant to trust and share with a stranger. Instead of only meeting with them once, she scheduled a second meeting (with food again!) to ask them more specific questions about their concerns about current services, types of services they wanted, and how they would want to be engaged in the programs in their community.

Assessment: After meeting with residents, Simone also met with a representative from the housing authority. The purpose of the meeting was to hear from their perspective what they thought the issues were in their high rise. After listening to both sides of the issue, Simone concluded that there were fewer programs because of the funding cuts. Without the resources the hire people to lead the activities, the housing authority reduced their programming without explaining this to the residents because they thought they would receive additional funds from a recent grant application. The grant was not funded and the housing authority is looking for other resources. However, this information had not been shared.

Planning: Simone facilitated a lunch meeting with both the housing authority representative and the residents. Each side had the opportunity to hear each other's concerns about the situation during the meeting. Although the high rise had a residents council as their "voice" to the housing authority, it had declining participation and was not very active. This was the first time the two groups of stakeholders met with an outside organization, and the group met a few more times to develop a plan of action. The group's plan included reactivating the residents council so that the communication between the residents and the housing authority could be improved. As a result of the re-activated residents council, the residents and the housing authority developed a plan for increased resident engagement in which they pilot tested a program that is resident led.

Implementation: Simone introduced the residents and the housing authority representative to a professor in the nutrition department at a local university to explore a partnership to develop a pilot project. After months of planning, the residents implemented their first activity, a nutrition education program. The housing authority, residents, and the professor and her students collaborated on an 8-week program that focused on providing information about health and nutrition (the area of interest selected by the residents) and opportunities for cooking demonstrations and recipe sharing.

Evaluation: The group met weekly for eight sessions, and at the end of each session the participants were asked questions about what they liked about sessions, what they would improve, and how they would use the information that was provided. The feedback from the sessions was used to improve subsequent sessions. Prior to the start of the program, and after the final session, they were also asked about how well they thought their relationship with the housing authority improved, what worked well, and what could be improved.

Termination: At the conclusion of the nutrition project, Simone, the housing authority, and the residents held a debriefing session to assess how well the goals of the program were met. They then discussed their plans for moving forward and the options for other programs and funding opportunities to support other types of programs. Although Simone's formal role with the project ended with its conclusion, she and her organization have remained a community partner.

Simone's example demonstrates how the model can be applied. Throughout this workbook you will have opportunities to apply the model in each chapter. The book is organized into the following chapters:

Chapter 2 will present client engagement within the context of groups, communities, and organizations. This overview will include the similarities and differences between engagement at the micro, mezzo, and macro levels of intervention. For example, how can a social worker initiate the process when entering a community to develop a partnership? The chapter will conclude with an exercise in which students will identify strategies for engagement in a case study about entry into a community.

The process of identifying problems in partnership with stakeholders in communities and organizations will be the focus of chapter 3. How to use engagement skills to assess and identify problems to start developing a plan for actions will be described in detail. Content examples include the types of information that should be collected, who should be part of the assessment process, and how to analyze the available information.

Chapter 4 will discuss how to move from assessment to planning. Data analysis techniques will be discussed as strategies to disseminate the information to stakeholders. Part of the planning will include content and both process (how to facilitate discussion and consensus) and outcome (developing common goals and objectives) strategies that use micro skills. This chapter's exercise will be developing a plan (i.e., developing goals and a realistic, feasible timeline) based on the problem identified in chapter 3. This chapter will provide students with content on how to put a plan into action. The focus will be on project/program management and monitoring, and topics will include resource management (both human and financial) accountability, reporting to stakeholders, and knowing when to make adjustment to an initial plan. The strategies associated with implementations are the focus of chapter 5.

Assessing and evaluating progress toward goals will be examined in chapter 6. A brief overview of evaluation designs will be included to provide a framework for students' understanding of how they can assess progress—similar to what they would do when working with an individual client.

Ending the professional relationship is part of the generalist model, and chapter 7 will focus on the differences and similarities for termination when working with individuals compared to communities and organizations. For example, termination of the professional relationship with an individual client may be making use of referrals while a community-level termination may be developing a leadership succession plan after the social worker is no longer working with the community. Termination is an opportunity to assess the results of the project or effort and how "success" is measured needs to be defined. Follow-up with individual clients is used to touch base with clients to see what is working and may not be working as well since the termination of the professional relationship. At the macro, level, this same type of follow-up can be done after time has passed to see what has been useful and effective and to identify any additional supports that may be needed. Chapter 8 is an opportunity to apply the model to a single case study from a stakeholder perspective.

This book is intended to "bridge" the gap between the skills and knowledge learned for social work practice with individuals and groups and how they are used in macro settings. Each chapter will build on each other to show the generalist model though a macro social work practice perspective. Through exercises and reflection activities, students will be able to understand how the skills used with working with individuals can be can be applied in a macro context.

REFERENCE

Reisch, M. (2018). *Macro social work practice: Working for change in a multicultural society*. San Diego, CA: Cognella.

CHAPTER 2

Engagement: Facilitate Relationship Development and Build Rapport With Clients/ Key Stakeholders

LEARNING OBJECTIVES

The goal of this chapter is to identify the skills social workers can use to engage clients and stakeholders and to build rapport. Students will have the opportunity to review and apply the following skills in micro and macro scenarios:

- Observation and awareness of verbal and nonverbal communication
- Active listening
- Diverse communication styles
- Balancing honesty, conflict resolution, negativity, resistance, and failure with respect

INTRODUCTION

> *"Hello, My name is [fill in the blank] and it is nice to meet you."*

This is greeting often used to introduce ourselves when we meet someone new. It is intended to be informative (letting them know who we are) and an initial attempt to build rapport. A greeting as simple as this is an example of how we can initiate engagement with another person. During the engagement phrase of the generalist model, the focus is on building relationships that will allow social workers to be partners in the change process. The key to developing these relationships is the ability to use our interpersonal skills to effectively communicate. Specific interpersonal skills that essential to relationship building are as follows:

Observation and Awareness of Verbal and Nonverbal Communication

Communication does not only involve verbally sharing ideas. It also includes observing and responding to facial expressions, the tone of what is said, body language (e.g., crossing arms across chest), and emotional responses. In order to make sure that are not only giving messages, we need to be able to assess how well we are receiving them.

Active Listening

Active listening is not the same as listening. Listening is where you hear the words that are spoken; active listening is when you not only hear the words but also the meaning behind what has been said. Imagine that a client is describing his or her experiences with a service provider: "I cannot be believe I had to wait 30 minutes and when I finally met with the social worker she rushed me through the meeting." Here are three potential responses:

1. "Wow, the agency must have been really busy; at least you were able to get an appointment."

2. "It's good that you were able to meet with someone."

3. "You sound like you felt you should not have had to wait that long to only be rushed once you were finally able to meet with the social worker. This sounds like it was frustrating for you."

Although the first two responses may be efforts to help the client not take the situation personally, it did not acknowledge how the client is feeling. Response #3 reflects what the social worker heard about the experience and the feelings/reactions associated with it.

Diverse Communication Styles

Communication styles vary and are influenced by culture and individual personality. Cultural nuances such as maintaining a respectful distance, shaking hands, and direct contact need to be considered during interactions so as to not appear disrespectful or unaware. Also, social workers must be mindful of the language and terminology (such as slang) that are used because they may not be the same as how the client or community refers to an experience, object, or experience.

Balancing Honesty, Conflict Resolution, Negativity, Resistance, and Failure With Respect

Part of being a social worker is the ability to be clear and direct in our communication so that our messages are received accurately. In addition, social workers are also expected to use their communication to resolve conflict by diffusing tension, working with individuals and groups to see an issue or conflict from each perspective, and asking probing questions to identify the reasons for resistance to change/ideas and exploring the factors that contribute to less-than-successful outcomes.

APPLYING THE SKILLS

In micro practice, these skills are used to develop trust with clients so that they will comfortable sharing their experiences and perceptions of the problems that are of concern. Although the interviewing process may be a friendly exchange, it is not a social visit, and the reason for the meeting needs to be clear. During the initial meeting, the client and the social worker should be clear about the purpose of why they are meeting, the expectations of the partnership, and the next steps for moving forward. The interaction is focused on learning more about the situation so that a formal assessment of the problem can be made.

Asking the right questions is essential for getting an accurate understanding of the identified issue or problem. Using a blend of closed and open-ended questions should be used to get responses that are both descriptive and insightful. Closed questions are used to get specific information (e.g., "How many children do you have?") while open-ended questions are used to further the discussion by giving the client the opportunity to respond in their own words with additional depth (e.g., "What would you like for me to know about your children"?).

Awareness of nonverbal and verbal communication and active listening can be demonstrated by acknowledging what you have heard and any relevant observations. For example, if you ask a person "How many children do you have?" and they are hesitant to respond and their voice lowers to a whisperr you may want to follow up with the statement, "It seems like asking about your children may be a sensitive topic for you because when I asked how many children you have, you hesitated and lowered your voice and avoided looking at me. What would you like to share about your children and reaction to my question?"

This example also demonstrates how a social worker can respond to topic with sensitivity to what appears to be an uncomfortable situation. Instead of asking multiple questions in succession that may feel more like an interrogation, the response acknowledges the observed nonverbal communication. The response does not allow the individual to move past what was said (or in this case, not said) without addressing it, but the response is supportive and moves toward the next question to initiate further discussion.

The process is the same for macro practice, but instead of working with an individual or a family system, the engagement is with a group as part of a meeting. Your role in the meeting or gathering of individuals is to facilitate an interview with multiple individuals simultaneously. The same principles apply but you are managing a conversation with multiple perspectives.

Engagement Skills: Micro and Macro Applications

	Micro	Macro
Observation and awareness of verbal and nonverbal communication	"I noticed that you have been tapping your foot and speaking very quickly. Are you nervous about anything?"	"I noticed that some members of the group have started talking and making faces at each other and rolling their eyes when I mentioned the name of the property manager. Since I am not from here, can you tell me what this means?"
Active listening	"Thank you for telling me about your experience with the other service provider. It sounds like you were disappointed in how they treated you."	"Thank you for sharing your experiences with the property manager. It sounds like most of you have had some type of interaction in which you felt disrespected. Would anyone else like to add how they may have felt disrespected?"
Diverse communication styles	"I understand that some of the terms associated your condition may not be clear to you. Please feel free to ask any questions for clarification."	"I understand that we may be using different terms to describe places or things in your neighborhood. Please let me know if I am using terms to describe what is going on here incorrectly."
Balancing honesty, conflict resolution, negativity, resistance, and failure with respect	"I am sorry to hear that you are upset about the way you were treated, but in order for us to work together, I ask that you stop yelling so that I can be sure to respond to your concerns."	Thank you for sharing your frustrations with me. However, in order for me hear everyone I am going to ask that you stop yelling."

EXERCISE: APPLYING ENGAGEMENT SKILLS IN MICRO AND MACRO PRACTICE SETTINGS

Instructions: Review each scenario and identify how you would use your engagement skills to begin building rapport. If you would like practice applying the skills, you can role play each scenario with one of your fellow students based on the responses you have selected.

Scenario A: A woman has been referred to the prenatal program at your agency. She is 30 years old single, and does not have health insurance because she recently lost her job. She is embarrassed to seek assistance because she has always been able to afford to take care of herself. When she first arrives for her meeting, she does not make direct eye contact and constantly looks around the waiting room as if she is trying to avoid seeing anyone she might know. When you ask her why she has come to see you, she states, "I am here because my doctor made me and am not even sure I really need your help."

1. What is a response you would use to acknowledge the verbal and nonverbal communication?

2. What are two responses you would use to demonstrate your active listening to the client?

    a.

    b.

3. What communication style differences would you consider in your initial discussion with your client?

4. You want to learn more about the woman's background so that you can begin collecting information that will be useful to you as begin to develop an understanding of her situation. Select one closed question and one open-ended question to further the discussion:

    Closed response:

    Open-ended response:

Scenario B: You have been invited by a group of community residents who are concerned about the condition of their neighborhood. You are attending the meeting with 20 residents. They have complained to the city about the abandoned houses, overgrown yards, and trash that is on the main road. They are frustrated and angry because they do not feel the city is paying attention to them because they are not one of the higher income communities that they feel has benefitted from their connections to the mayor.

One man shouted, "No one cares about us because we are poor!" One woman, with tears in her eyes, stated that she is embarrassed to have people come to visit and "is sad to see how the neighborhood has gone downhill since [she] moved [t]here 10 years ago." Even though you were invited to the meeting by some members of neighborhood association, there were some members of the group that question why you were there, and one person asked, "Are you spy for the mayor's office?"

1. What is a response you would use to acknowledge the verbal and nonverbal communication within the group?

2. What are three responses you would use to respond to the group to demonstrate your active listening?

   a.

   b.

   c.

3. What communication style differences would you consider in your initial discussion with the group?

4. You want to learn more about the group and their experiences so that you can begin collecting information that will be useful to you as begin to develop an understanding of her situation. Select *two* closed questions and *two* open-ended questions to further the discussion:

   Closed response #1:

   Closed response #2:

   Open-ended response #1:

   Open-ended response #2:

SUMMARY

Relationship building is an essential component of social work practice that is necessary to engage individuals and groups in change processes. This is true for both micro and macro practice. Social workers who are aware of and know how to appropriately respond to communication within our interactions are better able to develop the rapport necessary for the assessment phase of the generalist model. If we are unable to ask the "right" and sometimes difficult questions, we will be limited in our ability to develop an accurate understanding of the situation or problem.

CHAPTER 3

Assessment: Develop an Initial Idea of the Factors That Contribute to the Current Situation or Presenting Problem

LEARNING OBJECTIVES

This chapter will identify processes associated with assessing individuals, organizations, communities, and institutions. The ecological perspective will be used as a framework to analyze the information obtained from the initial interview or group meeting as an initial step toward developing goals. At the end of this chapter students will be able to do the following:

- Identify the levels of intervention in the ecological perspective
- Apply the skills associated with assessment in micro and macro settings
- Identify potential sources of information and data that can be used in the assessment
- Develop goals based on the information obtained from an assessment

INTRODUCTION

After establishing the initial relationship with an individual or a group of stakeholders, the social worker will need to use his or her engagement skills to collect information about the situation. We use the information to "put the pieces together" in order to develop an initial idea of the factors that contributed to the current situation or problem. The information is then used as the rationale for the intervention or action step of the change process.

The Ecological Perspective: "Putting the Pieces of the Puzzle Together"

When working with individual clients, social workers use a bio-psychosocial or person in environment approach of why the situation or problem is occurring. These perspectives evaluate how various parts of an individual's systems interact. The ecological model provides the foundation for understanding the parts of the systems and how they interact to evaluate how the components of the client's life are connected at the micro, mezzo, and macro levels. The micro level includes biological and psychological characteristics. Biological characteristics include genetics, physical health, and nutrition, and examples of psychological characteristics include cognition, personality, and emotions. The mezzo level includes the interactions between the individual and the people of places that influence his or her daily life. Work and school settings, religious groups, friends, and family would be included in this level. The macro context has the broadest influence, but it provides a general societal context for understanding behavior. The broader community, organizations, societal norms, government, and the political system are included in this level. For example, if an individual comes to you because of issues related to what appears to be symptoms of depression, the social worker would ask questions about his or her physical health, interpersonal relationships and social support; the feelings he or she has been experiencing; changes in his or her life situation such a loss of employment, a death of a loved one, stress, and health insurance; and other factors that may be relevant. These factors represent both internal/micro (health, interpersonal relationships, feelings, death of a loved one) and mezzo/macro (social support, employment, and health care). Together, they represent the client's social history that will serve as a succinct summary of the client's experiences, characteristics (i.e., gender, age, ethnicity), and behaviors. The social history is also used to determine the severity of the problem and to develop an initial idea of why the situation or problem exists. Once this initial understanding of the problem is identified, the social worker uses his or her communication skills to learn the client's perception of the problem and existing strengths and resources that can be used as part of the change process. The assessment stage concludes with a tentative plan for moving forward and the goals that will be used to measure progress. However, it is important to note that assessment is an ongoing process. As additional information becomes available and the client shares more about his or her situation, the assessment can be updated to reflect this. Remaining flexible and open to receiving and incorporating this additional information is important so that additional details that can impact the treatment plan can be considered.

Goals

Goals are the desired outcome of the treatment or intervention plan and are developed in partnership with the client. "Good" goals are those that are specific, have a timeline, and are feasible.

Example: Mrs. Johnson is a client who has recently received her GED and completed a job training program. She is currently looking for employment and, based on her skills and qualifications, it is feasible for her to expect to find employment. Please see the examples of good, better, and best goal statements.

Goal #1: Mrs. Johnson will get a job. (Good)
Goal #2: Mrs. Johnson will get a job soon. (Better)
Goal #3: Mrs. Johnson will be obtain a full-time job within 3 months. (Best)

ASSESSMENT IN MACRO PRACTICE

For macro practice, the emphasis is on the broader social context. Instead of focusing on an individual and the systems he or she interacts with and influences, the emphasis is on communities, organizations, institutions, and political systems. Similar to the approach used in working with individual clients, the organizational or group management skills during this stage are identifying problems, articulating the issues, and developing specific goals from multiple stakeholders with diverse interests and need.

Identifying Problems

Instead of focusing on the interactions within an individual client system, the focus shifts to what we know about the issues the community or organization is experiencing. In order to develop an understanding of the problem(s), the social worker should ask how the problem is defined/perceived, what information or data can be used as evidence to support the perception of the problem (e.g., census, crime statistics, the number of people receiving a type of service), how long the problem has been occurring, and previous efforts to address the problem. This also requires that the social worker consider the impact of the actions of multiple stakeholders on various components of a community. For example, if crime is an issue in one part of the city, there may be spillover effect because the negative perceptions of that part of the city may extend to other areas. In addition, the social worker must also consider the impact the issue(s) has on the different populations in the community. Using the previous example, if a city is perceived as a high crime area, it may difficult to attract businesses to the community that will provide employment opportunities.

In order to gain an understanding of the problem, it is essential that those affected by the issue (residents, businesses, schools, law enforcement, politicians, etc.) are provided with opportunities to share their perspectives of the issues. Similar to working with individuals, it is important to hear from stakeholders how they define the problem because there needs to be a common understanding of how the problem is defined.

Articulating the Issues

When working with individual clients to ensure the social worker correctly "heard" what a client expressed, paraphrasing what was said (restating in your own words), summarizing the key points of the discussion, and reframing (presenting what was stated differently) are strategies that can be used. These same strategies are used in macro practice. The listening strategies can be used when acknowledging the different perspectives that have been expressed and identifying areas of common interest. It is not uncommon for there to be debate, and even at times an intense, heated discussed about the issues. However, this where active listening and conflict resolution skills are essential to move the discussion forward.

Developing Goals

Once the issues have been identified, the discussion needs to shift to what can be done about the issues and how the group will know when change has been achieved. Similar to working with clients, the social worker must engage the stakeholders in the goal development process. Part of the process includes taking an inventory of existing skills, assets, and any additional resources that are needed in order to determine what is realistic and feasible for the group to achieve as the outcomes to demonstrate their "success."

Assessment: Micro and Macro Overview

	Micro	Macro
Identifying the problem	The client's social history	The community and organization's history Policy analysis (formulation, implementation, and revision)
Skills	Analyze the client situation Identify existing assets and strengths Identify potential barriers	Analyze the interests and commitments of different individuals and groups Identify existing assets and strengths Identify sources of power and influence Identify areas of potential conflict
Examples of data sources	The client Client medical and service records Service providers Persons familiar with the client situation (e.g., family) as appropriate	Census data Crime data Employment and labor data Funding sources Student test scores Information about services provided Legislative and organizational policies
Goal setting	Developed in partnership with the client Specific and feasible Based on a timeline	Developed in partnership with the stakeholders Specific and feasible Based on a timeline

EXERCISE: ASSESSING A PROBLEM

Instructions: Review the scenarios and develop a strategy for learning more about the issue.

Scenario A: Mark is a social worker at a child advocacy organization and part of the organization's mission is to ensure that children in the community receive a quality pre-K (pre-kindergarten) education. After meeting a school administrator who shared her concern about decreased enrollment and the challenges facing lower-income children in the community, you and your director thought it would be a good idea to talk to parents and teachers to see if (a) they consider it an issue and (b) if it is an issue, why is it happening. Mark's director, Jennifer, will meet with the teachers, and he will meet with the parents to learn more about what they think about the education and resources available in the community for their preschool kids. Imagine that you are

Mark and are preparing to work with the parents. Your responses will develop an initial assessment plan for this part of the project.

1. Although you have been assigned to meet with parents, what, if any, stakeholders would you would invite to the meeting? Why do you think their perspective is important?

2. What are three initial questions you would ask the group? Please include your rationale for each question.

   Question #1: _____

   Rationale: _____

   Question #2: _____

   Rationale: _____

   Question #3: _____

   Rationale: _____

3. What data would you collect to learn more about the potential issue(s)?

4. What are your next steps to move from assessment to goal setting?

   a.

   b.

   c.

Scenario B: Jennifer is the director of child advocacy organization and is working with Mark on the school project. She is meeting with the teachers and other school administrators to learn more about how they perceive the problem from a system perspective. She wants to learn how the school system itself impacts enrollment and the experiences of the lower-income children in the school. Imagine that you are Jennifer and are preparing to work with the school teachers and administrators. Your responses will develop an initial assessment plan for this part of the project.

1. Although you have been assigned to meet with parents, what, if any, stakeholders would you would invite to the meeting? Why do you think their perspective is important?

2. What are three initial questions you would ask the group? Please include your rationale for each question.

Question #1: _____

Rationale: _____

Question #2: _____

Rationale: _____

Question #3: _____

Rationale: _____

3. What data would you collect to learn more about the potential issue(s)?

4. What are your next steps to move from assessment to goal setting?

   a.

   b.

   c.

SUMMARY

Assessing client systems and the factors contributing to the current problems and issues requires critical thinking and analysis skills to pull the multiple sources of information into a cohesive history/background that will provide a context for developing an intervention or social change plan. It is important to remember that assessments are not static, and as new information becomes available it needs to be considered as part of the ongoing process of observing, asking questions, and actively listening to what is said as well as what is not explicitly stated.

CHAPTER 4

Planning: Use the Information from the Assessment to Develop a Plan for Action With Clearly Defined Goals

LEARNING OBJECTIVES

This chapter will present strategies for aligning the information obtained during the assessment with the resources and people as part of strategic plan for change. At the end of this chapter, students will able to do the following:

- Describe the characteristics of appropriate goals
- Conduct a SWOT analysis
- Develop goals and objectives based on the SWOT analysis

INTRODUCTION

After taking the time to engage clients and stakeholders to build rapport and develop an initial understanding of why the situation is occurring, it is time to move into the planning stage of setting strategic goals and identifying strategies to achieve the goals.

Planning: "Now What?"

As discussed in chapter 3, goals are the intended outcome of the intervention or change strategy. During the assessment stage, the information is used to develop an *initial* plan. During planning, the goals and the way to move toward achieving them is more clearly defined. To provide an outline of the steps necessary to track and monitor progress toward goals and objectives, the actions that will be done are used to provide a clear understanding of the plan and the expectations.

In micro practice, the treatment or intervention plan is focused on coordinating the resources to support the selected intervention. Common social work interventions include case management, referrals for services, and counseling. The selected interventions are aligned with the problems identified in the social history. If a client has multiple problems to address, it is important to not overwhelm him or her with too many goals and objectives. Goals and objectives are manageable when they are broken down into smaller steps. Starting with one or two goals is a good strategy to avoid making the planning stage too overwhelming. Remember, goals should be specific, be feasible, and have a timeline.

Example: Jason is a 27-year-old male. His social history revealed that he exhibited symptoms associated with depression and has had a history of depressive episodes since his teens. It was noted in his history that he was socially isolated with very few friends and did not taken medication consistently for his depression when he was a teen.

During the initial meeting he described changes in his life situation (recent loss of his job and a loved one) that appear to have exacerbated his symptoms. The social worker referred him to a psychiatrist for in-depth assessment of the depressive symptoms to evaluate the severity and to determine if medication is needed as part of the treatment plan because of his prior history. After his psychological evaluation, the doctor prescribed him antidepressants to balance his affect, mood, and emotions. He returned to the social worker for his therapeutic sessions.

Goal: Jason will make new friends and take his medication as prescribed.
Objective 1: Jason will attend three social events a month.
Objective 2: Jason will make at least one contact at each social event.
Objective 3: Jason will take his medication as prescribed every day for at least 1 year.

This goal is not only overwhelming but is it poorly written because it is two goals in one. Since Jason has had a history of social isolation, he is not likely going to go to three social events a month, and making a contact at each one. Although a year is indicated at the timeline for objective 3, it is too far in the future and may seem daunting to achieve. Here is a revision:

Goal 1: Jason will take his medication as prescribed for 1 month.
Objective 1: Jason will fill his prescription.

Objective: 2: Jason will use a calendar (either hard copy or phone) to track when he takes his medication.

Objective 3: Jason will set an alarm as a reminder to take his medication.

Objective 4: Jason will take his medication at the scheduled time and in the correct dosage.

Although developing a support network will benefit Jason, the priority is to stabilize his mood and depressive symptoms while he is attending his counseling sessions. The timeframe is limited to only 30 days for his medication adherence to become a habit. This is also a way for Jason to experience success early and gain confidence in his ability to achieve additional goals.

PLANNING IN MACRO PRACTICE

Planning in macro practice is strategic and combines activities that support process and outcomes. The process refers to *how* the effort is planned and implemented. The outcomes are the *what*—the results of the effort. Similar to using the social history as the foundation for the intervention plan, macro practice uses strategic analyses as the foundation for the macro change effort. A commonly used strategy is a SWOT analysis: strengths, weaknesses, opportunities, and threats. This strategy allows groups, organizations, and communities to use the information in the assessment to evaluate what should be priority in their plans. Strengths and weakness are internal influences, and opportunities and threats are external. The table that follows includes examples of each category.

	Strengths	**Weaknesses**
Internal factors	**Positive attributes** Financial resources History in the community Engaged community partners A history of success	**Negative attributes** Limited financial resources Conflict among partners Low visibility in the community Instability Past failures
	Opportunities	**Threats**
External factors	**Factors the contribute to success** Funders and institutions that support your effort or mission Developing a niche (specialization) in the social service delivery system Momentum for and interest in mobilizing for an advocacy effort	**Factors out of anyone's control but that can have an impact** Major funding leaves the community or no longer provides support A new organization is created that provides similar services Policy changes

The SWOT analysis can be used to guide planning meetings because it provides a framework for analyzing the information that has been collected about an issue, organization, or community.

MACRO PRACTICE GOAL SETTING

The main difference between goal setting in micro and macro practice is the unit of analysis: individuals versus groups, organizations, and communities. The goals should also be manageable, specific, feasible, and on a timeline. The SWOT analysis provides an opportunity to develop goals that meet these criteria.

Example: Phoenix Rising is a residential facility that has been providing services to the community for more than 15 years. A recent SWOT analysis revealed that a potential threat is the continued reduction in state funding. The leadership of the organization developed the following goals and objectives for the organization:

Goal: Diversify the organization's funding strategy by the end of 2020.
Objective 1: Identify at least three non-government funding sources by May 2019.
Objective 2: Contact the funding sources to schedule meetings (or attend scheduled webinars) to learn more about the application process by June 2019.
Objective 3: Prepare and submit grant applications to at three new funding sources by December 2019.

These goals and objectives support a plan to seek new funding sources within a specific and feasible timeline, with outcomes that will support the overall plan to diversify the funding strategy.

EXERCISE: DEVELOPING A PLAN

Instructions: Review the scenario. Develop a SWOT analysis and plan for addressing the issues.

Scenario: Jennifer and Mark (from chapter 3) worked with the stakeholders to develop an assessment of the declining pre-K school enrollment and the challenges the lower-income students were experiencing. The group included the following information in the assessment report:

1. The population in the city has declined but the population of preschool age children has remained constant.

2. The educators have observed that more children are coming to school hungry and without school supplies.

3. Since transportation is not provided for pre-K students, some parents have decided to use other child options (e.g., family members, in-home child care), instead of sending them to the schools since they do not have reliable transportation.

4. The parents are committed to their children and providing them with the best preparation for entry into kindergarten.

5. Although the parents are committed to their children and their education, some parents are not sure of the benefits of a formal pre-K program because other day care providers are more convenient and accessible on evenings and weekends.

6. Most of the teachers have taught at the school for at least 10 years; the principal has been at the school for 15 years.

7. The school recently received a grant from the U.S. Department of Education to develop a 5-year project to examine the educational outcomes of the students in their school as they transition into elementary school. This project provides additional learning resources and supportive students to enhance their age-appropriate development.

8. The school has the perception that they are not engaged in the broader community and do not participate in many community events.

9. The school in the process of developing their social media presence and incorporating technology into their teaching model.

10. Due to the popularity of the pre-K program in other schools, the state recently implemented a lottery system in an effort to distribute enrollment more evenly among the schools to avoid schools with low enrollment and overcrowding.

SWOT: Use the following table to complete your analysis.

Internal factors	Strengths	Weaknesses
External factors	Opportunities	Threats

1. What are the primary issues that need to be addressed? Briefly discuss your reasons for selecting them.

2. How can the strengths and opportunities be used as part of change strategy?

3. How can the impact of the weaknesses and threats be reduced?

4. Identify at least two goals for this group to address:

   Goal 1: _____

   Objective 1: _____

   Objective 2: _____

   Objective 3: _____

   Goal 2: _____

   Objective 1: _____

   Objective 2: _____

   Objective 3: _____

SUMMARY

Planning is the road map for any intervention or change strategy. It provides checkpoints (objectives) that make sure you are on track to reach your destination (the goal). The plan, whether it is an individualized treatment plan or a plan for social change and advocacy, is also used to outline what is expected as the outcome of the effort. It provides everyone with an understanding of what will be done in preparation for the action phase in which roles, responsibilities, and activities will be specified.

CHAPTER 5

Implementation: Follow Through on the Action Plan and Monitor Progress Toward Goal Achievement

LEARNING OBJECTIVES

The goal of this chapter is to apply the skills learned in previous chapters to develop a plan for monitoring the progress of the macro intervention. At the conclusion of this chapter, students will be able to do the following:

- Describe the differences and similarities in monitoring processes associated with micro and macro practice
- Identify strategies used to monitor progress during implementation
- Develop a plan to monitor the progress of a coalition's activities and strategies in a social change scenario

INTRODUCTION

After assessing the situation, developing an initial idea of the contributing factors, identifying targets of change, and establishing goals to guide the effort, it is finally time to put the plan into action.

"Let's Do It!"

This stage of the generalist model is action oriented and dynamic. Although the planning stage provides a guide for how to move forward, it is not unusual to revise the plan in response to changes in the client's situation. As a result, it is important to carefully monitor progress toward goal achievement in order to change or revise the plan if it does not appear to be progressing. In micro practice, this is client centered and the treatment plan is used to hold the client and the social work accountable for what activities and tasks they agreed to complete. Access to resources, social support, coping and problem-solving skills, substance abuse issues, and mental health status are examples of factors that can influence the "successful" implementation of the treatment plan. Displaying empathy and asking open-ended and probing questions are the social work skills that are effective when exploring the factors that influence implementation.

Monitoring

Monitoring is an ongoing review of how a plan is being implemented (the types of services used, the decisions that are made, how much and what type of resources are used, and the behavior, policy, and program changes that have been made). In order to manage a treatment or social change/advocacy plan, documentation is an important component of the process to maintain records of what has taken place.

Monitoring: Micro Practice

When working with individuals, the individual treatment goals are described in a service contact or agreement that summarizes how the social worker and client plan to work together. The contract is useful because it is a written summary of what behaviors or activities the client will do in support of the identified goals. Information about the type of referrals used, the number of sessions attended, documentation from other providers, a cost summary of the services provided, and observable changes in behavior, knowledge, and skills are examples of information that can be used to review and monitor client progress.

Monitoring: Macro Practice

In macro settings, monitoring is a combination of process and outcome factors. The process factors consider *how* the project is implemented while the outcomes focus on *what* is achieved. The organizational and partnership goals specify the targets for change. Similar to the service contract with individual clients, memorandums of agreement or partnership agreements specify what each organization will contribute to the collaborative effort. Instead of client notes, meeting agendas and minutes are ways to document what decisions have been made and the next steps that are needed for follow-up. Progress toward achieving goals can be tracked by measuring changes in the selected outcomes (e.g., increased service providers, less crime, increased funding). It is also important to track how the effort's spending aligns with the proposed budget.

Monitoring Examples During Implementation

Micro	Macro
• Individual treatment goals	• Organizational and partnership goals
• Service contract	• Memorandums of agreement or partnership agreements (collaboration)
• Client referrals	
• Frequency of sessions/visits	• Meeting minutes and documentation
• Client records and documentation	• Resource allocation
• Treatment costs	• Are the resources being used
• Changes in scores on behavior, skill, and knowledge assessment measures	Are the resources used effective?
	Are the resources used efficiently?
• Progress reports	• Are the resources adequate?
	• Changes in organizational and community data used to assess outcomes and impact
	• Progress reports

Collaboration is the process of two or more individuals or entities working together to achieve mutually achieved goals. In macro practice, a common type of collaboration is a coalition. A coalition is "an organization or organizations that share articulated social or political change goals and [are] characterized by dynamic tensions" (Reisch, 2018, p. 157). Coalitions build on their collective power and resources to achieve the selected goals by engaging a broad and diverse group of stakeholders. They are time limited, clearly articulate how they are defining the issues, share a set of values, and have leadership that is able to represent their positions and interests outside of the group and facilitate decision making within the group.

In macro practice, internal (stakeholders, group structure) and broader external influences (economic changes, politics) can influence implementation. To further explore how these issues affect implementation, strategic, political, and administrative skills will need to be applied in order to facilitate the development of the collaborative partnerships necessary to complete the work. Strategic and political skills reflect the social worker's ability to assess the interests and commitments of different stakeholder groups; continuously identify sources of power and minimize the threat of adversaries; facilitate group processes that will promote cohesion and collaboration within one's group, organization, and constituency while working as part of larger coalitions; and identify and address conflict.

Macro practice administrative and management skills are needed in this stage to provide oversight to the organizational and community-focused activities within a coalition. These skills are necessary to match the activities in the plan with the appropriate resources (development and allocation), facilitate group decision making, and establish effective working relationships that respect differences and time management.

Communication

Clear and consistent communication is essential during implementation because each stakeholder needs to be aware of how the effort is progressing. This should include maintaining accurate records, minutes, and reports for accountability in order to keep the strategy focused and on task. In order to do so, it may be necessary to use different communication styles and formats to deliver the information. For example, if presenting a progress report to a funder, the report would be more formal and include data that shows how the activities funded by the grant reflect the intended goals of the project and alignment between the proposed and actual budget. If the target audience is community members, a newsletter, a post in the neighborhood social media group page, or an e-mail blast may be the most appropriate way to communicate project updates.

EXERCISE: PROGRAM IMPLEMENTATION AND MONITORING

Instructions: Review the goals you developed in chapter 4 as part of the implementation plan. Develop a plan to monitor the group (coalition's) efforts during the implementation.

1. What is the target for change? (What will your plan address)?

2. What are the primary goals for the plan? (What do you want to achieve?)

3. What is the timeline for the plan? (How long will it take to achieve the goals)?

4. How will you monitor the plan? (How will you know you are on track to achieve the goals?)

5. What specific monitoring strategies will you use? (What information will you use to track the progress toward the goals?)

Check all that apply and indicate your rationale for selecting each one.

Monitoring Strategies

	Yes	No	Rationale
Organizational and partnership goals and objectives			
Memorandums of agreement or partnership agreements (collaboration)			
Meeting minutes and documentation			
Resource allocations			
Changes in organizational and community data used to assess outcomes and impact			
Progress reports			

6. What is your communication plan? (How will you communicate with internal and external stakeholder about the coalition's progress?)

7. Who are the stakeholders you will include in your communication plan? List them.

   a.

   b.

   c.

   d.

   e.

8. How will you communicate with these stakeholder group? List three specific strategies you plan to use and include the rationale for why think they are appropriate for the selected group.

   a.

   b.

   c.

SUMMARY

Implementation builds on the previous stages of the generalist model by moving from information gathering to action. Since there are multiple activities taking place simultaneously to support the larger strategy, monitoring is essential. Without monitoring, it will be easy to lose focus and potentially hinder progress toward goal achievement. An essential component of monitoring is clear, consistent, and communication that is targeted to the community stakeholders involved in and affected by the effort as part of the overall effort so that all can remain informed and engaged.

REFERENCE

Reisch, M. (2018). *Macro social work practice: Working for change in a multicultural society.* San Diego, CA: Cognella.

CHAPTER 6

Evaluation: Evaluate Progress Toward Goal Achievement and the Processes Used to Implement the Strategy

LEARNING OBJECTIVES

The goal of this chapter is to identify evaluation strategies that can be used to assess how well the desired goals have been met and how they were achieved. At the end of this chapter students will be able to do the following:

- Distinguish between process and outcome evaluation in macro practice
- Select appropriate outcomes for an evaluation of a macro practice scenario
- Develop an evaluation plan that incorporates process and outcome assessment

INTRODUCTION

Evaluation is the stage of the model in which we assess to what extent the treatment goals have been achieved. Although evaluation is presented late in the model, it should be addressed in earlier discussions about goals so that the specific outcomes that will be assessed are clearly defined.

"How Are We Doing/How Did We Do?"

Evaluation examples include measures of changes in behavior, skills, and attitudes as the result of interventions and client satisfaction surveys. In macro practice, the analytic skills can be used to not only evaluate goal/task achievement (outcome evaluation) but also the processes used to implement the strategy (process evaluation). By assessing both tasks and process goals, social workers can gain insight into what characteristics of the strategy (e.g., working relationships, resource allocation, conflict management, and communication) facilitated or hindered outcomes.

In clinical practice, the evaluation is focused on what has changed for the client as the result of the intervention that was used. The goals are a good way to determine if change has happened. For example, if the goal was for the client to obtain full-time employment in 6 months, you can easily assess if it this has happened within the timeline. In addition to determining if the goals have been met, this is also a good time to evaluate what factors contributed to or prevented the client from meeting his or her goals. If a client was successful in finding employment, his or her interview preparation and updated resume may have significantly contributed to the job search. In contrast, if the client was late to an interview and did not complete the suggested job training program because of inconsistent transportation, these would be barriers that would need to be considered.

Macro Practice Evaluation

Macro practice can be evaluated at the organizational, community, and policy levels of intervention. Organizations can assess their overall functioning, service delivery, and resource management. Organizations can either conduct an assessment of the entire organization or focus on a specific program. Community evaluation can assess a coalition's advocacy efforts for social change or the impact of an intervention (e.g., a health and wellness campaign) on the behavior, skills, and attitudes of those who are part of the community. Policy evaluation and analysis focuses on the processes used to pass the legislation and the intended and unintended consequences of the policy. Although the context of the evaluation may be different, there are common elements of a macro-focused evaluation. Since evaluation is an ongoing process, a combination of short-term, mid-term, and long-term results should be included as part of the overall design.

Evaluation Designs

Evaluation and the monitoring processes described in the previous chapter are closely related because they rely on a systematic review of how the plan is functioning as intended. In macro practice, using process and outcome evaluation can provide a balanced perspective of what happened and what the effect was. When assessing outcomes, how they will be measured must be clearly identified. For

Reflection 1:

1. After learning about monitoring (chapter 5) and evaluation, what do you think are the differences between them?

2. How are they similar?

3. How do you think they can be used together as part of the overall effort/plan?

individual clients, data can include assessment tools to measure concepts such as depression, anxiety, and stress if the outcome is a reduction in symptoms. In macro practice, the stakeholders will have to clearly state how they will measure success. For example, if the outcome is to increase the number of child care programs in a certain community, how many new programs would be considered successful? Or, in a program evaluation, how will the organization define improved client outcomes? The questions should be a combination of open-ended and closed questions. During a process evaluation open-ended questions (similar to how they are used in the assessment stage) are a way to obtain deeper insight into the how, what, and why of the activities that took place and of the selected strategies. Closed questions are useful for collecting data from surveys about demographics or the presence or absence of a condition or issue.

Examples of Process and Outcome Evaluation Questions (Reisch, 2019)

Process	Outcome
How were decisions made?	Were the goals achieved?
Was the decision-making process inclusive?	What were the targets of change?
How were stakeholders engaged in the decision-making process?	What changes were observed (directly and indirectly)?
What resources were used?	What were the effects of the effort/ community intervention?
What were the strengths of the collaboration?	What goals were not met?
What were the challenges of the collaboration?	What are the sustainable results?

EXERCISE: CREATE AN EVALUATION PLAN

Using the intervention you developed in from chapter 6, create an evaluation plan that includes process and outcome evaluation.

1. Proposed process evaluation: Identify three questions you think are appropriate to guide the process evaluation component.

    Question 1:

    Question 2:

    Question 3:

    a. What information will you collect to gain insight into the processes that were used to implement the plan? What questions will you ask to get this information?

    b. How will you define if the plan was successful? Include specific indicators you will use to define success.

2. Proposed outcome evaluation: Identify the key outcomes you will use to measure success and discuss why you have selected them.

    Outcome 1:

Rationale:

Outcome 2:

Rationale:

Outcome 3:

Rationale:

    c. What data/information will you collect to demonstrate if the outcome has been achieved?

SUMMARY

Evaluation is the systematic assessment of how well the goals were achieved and what was done to achieve them. Evaluation is an ongoing process that should can be used to assess short-term, middle term, and long-term goals as part of the monitoring processes described in the previous chapter. Consistent with the principles of collaboration (Reish, 2018), evaluation should incorporate the perspectives of stakeholders when defining how success will be defined and measured.

REFERENCE

Reisch, M. (2018). *Macro social work practice: Working for change in a multicultural society*. San Diego, CA: Cognella.

CHAPTER 7

Termination/Follow-Up: Formally End the Formal Professional Relationship and Make Appropriate Referrals for Follow-Up or Transition Plan

LEARNING OBJECTIVES

The goal of this chapter is to assist students with determining how and when to terminate the partnership. At the conclusion of this chapter students will be able to do the following:

- Determine when termination is appropriate in micro and macro settings
- Develop a plan for disseminating the results of the evaluation as a transition into the necessary steps to sustain the effort
- Identify the next steps for sustainability of the effort once the formal partnership has ended

INTRODUCTION

Unlike personal relationships. professional relationships should be defined for a specific period of time or purpose. Instead of abruptly ending the relationship, a discussion should be held about what happens once the professional relationship or partnership ends.

"It Has Been a Pleasure to Work With You"

Termination of the process used to describe when the professional working relationship ends. In micro practice, termination happens when one of the following takes place (Summers, 2016):

- The client's goals have been met and there is no further need for treatment or services
- The client dies or moves away
- The funding for the services is no longer available because the allocated resources for treatment have been used
- The client no longer wants to receive services and stops coming and/or formally initiates termination

Termination is an opportunity for closure. If the services were terminated because the goals were achieved, information is provided about supportive resources that may useful once the client is no longer working with a social worker. When a client stops coming for services, this is included as part of the case file, which documents the attempts to contact the client, what happened prior to termination, and any other relevant information about the case that should be included as part of the termination summary.

Termination in macro practice is defined by the goals of the coalition or other type of advocacy effort. By nature, coalitions are time limited and their termination is determined by what they were created to achieve. Once their purpose has been met, they conclude. Instead of the termination summary used in direct practice to close a class, a coalition's efforts conclude with a report of what was achieved, how it was done, and what is needed to sustain the effort. This is an opportunity to disseminate the results from the process and outcome evaluation results.

EXERCISE: CREATING A FOLLOW-UP PLAN

Instructions: You are part of the team working in the community to wrap up the coalition's efforts to address issues associated with increasing access to quality pre-K education. The group has completed the evaluation plan you developed in the previous chapter and it is now time to write the report to share the results as part of the dissemination and follow-up plan.

1. What information would you include in the report?

2. Who would you send a copy of the report? Why?

3. How would you disseminate it (e.g., post on a website, a newsletter, e-mail)?

4. Imagine that the goals of the coalition were met. Based on the goals that were achieved, what would you recommend for the next steps once the coalition ends it work?

SUMMARY

Termination is the formal "end" to professional relationship or collaborative partnership. Termination is an opportunity for closure and a plan for appropriate follow-up to support the achievements of the client or partnership after the intervention/advocacy efforts concludes. Without a plan for sustainability, it will be a challenge to maintain the achievements of the individual or partnership.

REFERENCE

Summers, N. (2015). *Fundamentals of case management: Skills for the Human Services.* (5th Ed). Belmont: Brooks/Cole.

CHAPTER 8

Conclusion: Putting It All Together

The goal of this chapter is apply what you have learned about each stage of the generalist process to a single case study. At the end of this chapter, students will be able to do the following:

- Identify a target for the intervention (change) plan
- Select strategies to assess, intervene, and evaluate the implementation of the plan
- Develop the next steps for termination and follow-up

THE CASE STUDY: "PUTTING IT ALL TOGETHER"

Instructions: Review the case of Pleasantville, USA, and use the prompts to develop a plan for change.

Pleasantville, USA

Pleasantville, USA is a seven-county metropolitan area with a population of approximately 300,000 that is experiencing both economic prosperity for some residents and economic hardship for others. For example, a new company moved its headquarters there and has contributed 25 new jobs to the local economy. These jobs have starting salaries between $40,000 to $75,000 per year. Although these are well-paying jobs, there are not a lot of them. In this community, the poverty rate is 17%, more than the state average of 10% and the national average of 12.3%. One of the largest challenges is the lack of jobs that more pay than minimum wage ($7.25 per hour), and even more importantly, a living wage. A living wage is the hourly rate that an individual must earn to support his or her family, if he or she is the sole provider and is working full time, 2,080 hours per year (Living Wage Calculator, 2019). In this metro area, the living wage is $10.98 per hour or a salary of approximately $22,830 per year.

This lack of employment has contributed to the poverty rates. For the families living in poverty, they are at a higher risk for lower educational achievement, involvement in the child welfare system, and substance use and abuse. Sunrise is a community with one of the highest poverty rates. A group of service providers and activists from Sunrise have come together to form a coalition to address these issues. Key stakeholders include the following:

One Hope
A nonprofit organization who has been serving the community for more than 20 years. They are a multi-service organization that focuses on children and families. Their services include child care, afterschool programs such a tutoring, job training for parents, and GED preparation.

Sunrise Community Development Corporation (CDC)
A CDC is a nonprofit organization that focuses on communities who are dealing with poverty. They are involved in variety of activities and services such as education, job training, and commercial and affordable housing development (National Alliance of Community Development Associations (NACDA), 2014). The Sunrise CDC was established 5 years ago as part of the city's strategic plan to create economic development initiatives that will be economic and employment opportunities to the area.

Poverty and Housing Advocate
Jennifer Smith works for a nonprofit organization as a poverty and housing advocate. She works as part of coalitions in the community to use her knowledge of and experience with legislative processes for policy change.

APPLYING THE GENERALIST MODEL

Part 1: Identify one of the stakeholder perspectives (One Hope, Sunrise CDC, or the poverty and housing advocate) you will assume as you develop a plan to address poverty-related issues. Briefly discuss what you think is that advocate's perspective of the issues it hopes the coalition will address.

Stakeholder perspective: _____

Perceptions of the issues:

_____

_____

_____

_____

ENGAGEMENT

Facilitate relationship development and build rapport with clients/key stakeholders.

Part 2: Based on the stakeholder perspective you selected, imagine that you are that in that role and are a co-facilitator of the coalition as you move into to the engagement phase of the generalist model. For this part of the exercise, respond to the following questions:

1. Who would you include as part of the effort and why?

2. How would you recruit and engage them to become part of the coalition?

3. What specific skills and techniques would you use to engage them after you have made initial contact?

ASSESSMENT

Develop an initial idea of the factors that contribute to the current situation or presenting problem.

Part 3: After bringing the members of the coalition together, consider how you will work with them to learn about the issues facing the community and define the problem or issue that will be the focus of the coalition's efforts.

1. Since poverty and its impact of the community is a broad issue, what data/information would you collect to develop an initial understanding of the issues and their impact on its residents? List three specific sources of information and briefly discuss why you have selected them.

   a.

   _____

   _____

   _____

   b.

   _____

   _____

   _____

   c.

   _____

   _____

   _____

2. What questions would you ask the coalition to facilitate a discussion that will identify the priorities and focus of the group?

   a.

   _____

   _____

b.

_____

_____

c.

_____

_____

3. How will you help the group come to an agreement on the priority issues and focus? How will you address potential conflicts in the group over individual versus collective interests?

_____

_____

_____

PLANNING

Use the information from the assessment to develop a tentative plan for action with clearly defined goals.

Part 4: Imagine that the group has identified three priority areas for the group's action plan.

1. List the three priorities.

   a. _____

   b. _____

   c. _____

2. Identify three goals (with objectives) based on the priorities that will be used to guide the coalition's efforts.

   Goal 1: _____

   Objective 1: _____

Goal 2: _____

Objective 2: _____

Goal 3: _____

Objective 3: _____

IMPLEMENTATION

Follow through on the action plan and monitor progress toward goal achievement.

Part 5: Based on the goal and objectives you identified, create an initial plan for how you will achieve the goals and objectives.

1. What *strategies and activities* will the coalition use to implement each of the goals and objectives from the previous section? Describe specific strategies and activities for each goal and objective.

    a. Goal and objective 1:

    b. Goal and objective 2:

    c. Goal and objective 3:

2. What *resources* will be needed to achieve each goal and objective? List the resources needed for each goal and objective and who will be responsible for each part of the plan. Include the rationale for each one.

    a. Goal and objective 1:

        i. Responsible stakeholder(s):

    b. Goal and objective 2:

        ii. Responsible stakeholder(s):

    c. Goal and objective 3:

        iii. Responsible stakeholder(s):

3. Describe your monitoring plan for the coalition's efforts to ensure the group is making progress toward achieving the goals. Include the information/data you will collect, who will collect it, and how often you will collect and review it.

_____

_____

_____

_____

_____

_____

EVALUATION

Evaluate progress toward goal achievement and the processes used to implement the strategy.

Part 6: Develop an evaluation plan for how the group will measure success.

1. What is the research design—process, outcome, or both? Explain the rationale for the design you have chosen.

_____

_____

_____

_____

_____

2. What types of data will you collect—quantitative, qualitative, or both?

_____

_____

_____

_____

_____

3. How will you determine success? Describe the indicators you will use to determine if the goals and objectives were achieved.

_____

_____

_____

_____

_____

TERMINATION AND FOLLOW-UP

_Formally end the formal professional relationship and make appropriate referrals for
follow-up or transition plan._

Part 7: Imagine two scenarios for the coalition after they complete the evaluation the
evaluation of their efforts:

1. They achieved their goals.

2. They _did not_ achieve their goals.

For each scenario, identify the next steps the groups will need to do after the formal
work of the coalition has ended. Briefly discuss your rationale for each step.

Scenario A: The coalition achieved their goals.

Step 1:

Step 2:

Step 3:

Step 4:

Scenario B: The coalition *did not* achieve their goals.

Step 1:

Step 2:

Step 3:

Step 4:

SUMMARY

At the conclusion of this chapter, the generalist model has been applied to a scenario from the perspective of your selected stakeholder: organization (One Hope), community (Sunrise CDC), or policy (poverty and housing advocate). Organizations, community, and policy are components of macro social work practice in which the generalist model can be used to bridge the gap between individuals and the larger systems in their physical, social, economic, and political environments.

REFERENCES

Living Wage Calculator. (2019). Retrieved from http://livingwage.mit.edu/

National Alliance of Community Development Associations (NACDA). (2014). What is a community development corporation? Retrieved from https://www.naceda.org/index.php?option=com_dailyplanetblog&view=entry&category=bright-ideas&id=25%3Awhat-is-a-community-development-corporation-&Itemid=171

www.ingramcontent.com/pod-product-compliance
Lightning Source LLC
Chambersburg PA
CBHW080427270326
41929CB00018B/3200